The Absence of Awful

By
Patricia A. Fisher

**Published by
ITSMEEE™ Industries
Aurora, CO
USA**

Patricia A Fisher

The Absence of Awful

Published by ITSMEEE™ Industries

All interior art by Patricia A. Fisher
Book layout and design by Patricia A. Fisher
Photography by D.H. Fisher
Book production and technical advice by D. H. Fisher
Cover production and design by D. H. Fisher
Edited by D. H. Fisher

Printed in the United States of America

First Edition

Library of Congress Control Number: 2012900662
ISBN: 978-0-9677231-8-1

Patricia A Fisher

Thank you
for being
a part of my
journey.

Patricia A.
Fisher

Patricia A Fisher

Other Titles by
Patricia A. Fisher

With Love ITSMEEE™
Copyright © 1997 by Patricia A. Fisher

With Love ITSMEEE™ II
Copyright © 1998 by Patricia A. Fisher

Introducing Number III, ITSMEEE™
Copyright © 1999 by Patricia A. Fisher

ITSMEEE™ On My Journey Home
Copyright © 1999 by Patricia A. Fisher
ITSMEEE™ Industries

Hello, ITSMEEE™ Again
Copyright © 2002 by Patricia A. Fisher
ITSMEEE™ Industries

ITSMEEE™ Beneath the Grey
An Autobiography
Copyright © 2003 by Patricia A. Fisher
ITSMEEE™ Industries

Other Titles (Continued)
By Patricia A. Fisher

From This Day Forward
Copyright © 2003 by Patricia A. Fisher
ITSMEEE™ Industries

I Want to LIVE!
Copyright © 2004 by Patricia A. Fisher
ITSMEEE™ Industries

Walk a Mile in Our Shoes
Copyright © 2005 by Patricia A. Fisher
ITSMEEE™ Industries

The Favor I Owe the World
Copyright © 2005 by Patricia A. Fisher
ITSMEEE™ Industries

Home Is Where We Park It!
Copyright © 2008 by Pat Fisher
Funhous Publishing

The Absence of Awful
Copyright © 2012 by Patricia A. Fisher
ITSMEEE™ Industries

Table of Contents:

Table of Contents Con't:

Table of Contents Con't:

Table of Contents Con't:

Patricia A Fisher

For This I Am Most Grateful

It seems that
Every morning now

I pray for
Peace of mind

It seems that
Every morning now

Depression's
What I find

Patricia A Fisher

I try to stay
So strong now

But after folks
I meet,

I'm scared
That they will hurt me

And then
I feel defeat

I find
I am suspicious

I don't know
What they want

What all do
They know of me

A trusted
Confidant?

Patricia A Fisher

Do they ask
Much more of me

Than I could
Ever give?

I wake up
In the mornings

Wanting
Not to live

So down I go
Most every time

Can I
Get out of bed?

Sometimes
It's two-thirty

Before I
Clear my head

Patricia A Fisher

Then out I go
To take that walk

That we do
Everyday

And look at
Lovely scenery

Enjoy it
If we may

For it takes
Such a warrior

Inside me
Just to live

To say hello
To someone

Is all that
I can give

Patricia A Fisher

But I have
Always had in me

This hope
Down deep inside

It seems to be
So deep in me

Yet many times
I've cried

So here we are
Together

My sweet love
And I

Living in
This moment

I don't want
To cry

Patricia A Fisher

I'm told I'm
Good at writing

I do it
In a bind

So here it is
My journaling

That I put in
A rhyme

I always seem
Quite able

To write
My fears away

And that is what
I'm doing

Again I start
To pray

Patricia A Fisher

My dearest
Heavenly Father

I sit here
With my man

You really, really
Blessed me

For this
I understand

Please don't let me
Waste it

The love we feel
Inside

For This
I Am Most Grateful

It cannot be
Denied

Patricia A Fisher

Recovery And

A Letter To

Heather

And

Laura

Patricia A Fisher

Where I come from
they taught us to wash
our hands after using
the bathroom.

Where I come from,
They taught us not to
Pee on our hands.

Author unknown

Tears Aren't Only For Sadness

I woke up this morning with the same old physical pain in my body.

Every morning is a challenge just to begin my daily walk toward the bathroom door. Each morning, when my feet touch the floor, I wonder if I will keep my balance. I wonder if my tired old knees will hold me up, as I begin that journey of only twenty feet.

As morning progresses, a lot of the pain subsides, and the day begins to look more promising.

This is when I feel fortunate to be alive. This is when I am free to smile in amazement, at all the many miracles of life.

Mom had a lot of pain in her waking hours. Each morning she would pull herself out of bed, head straight for the bottle of aspirin, then go on with her life. Even in her death, she gives me strength, because, like me, she was a warrior.

I lay there in the moments between dreams and wakefulness, and my dreams were of people caring about me.

We have a few good friends, but those people I speak of now are my health professionals.

They too believe in me and my writing. They contribute their hard earned money for copies of my books.

I catch myself beginning to say, "I love you", but I don't say it. It would mean that I'm crossing a professional line. So I say it in my books.

My dreams, this morning, were of compassion and respect.

I woke up smiling, in spite of the pain, and tears came to my eyes.

I lay there weeping and thankful for all these caring souls. This proves to me once again, that 'Tears Aren't Only for Sadness'.

A Fly Swatter

Is

A Real

Buzz Kill…

Patricia A Fisher

ROSES ARE RED

VIOLETS ARE BLUE

I'VE BEEN CUSSIN'

SINCE I WAS TWO

ROSES ARE RED

VIOLETS ARE BLUE

I WILL QUIT CUSSIN'

WHEN I'M WITH YOU

What Did One Peach
Say To
The Other Peach?

I Don't Know.

It Said:

I Feel Pity,
Oh So Pity!

What did one potato
Say to the other
potato?

I don't know…

It said:

See ya later
Tater!

Heather
(One of the caring souls)

God has blessed you many
times.
I feel it in my heart.
Even though God's done this,
I want to ask my part.

Please dear heavenly father,
Bless her once for me.
Bless all of her family.
Please just let them be,

Very easy to laughter,
Truth respect and love.
You are who can do this,
Straight from Heaven above.

Heather is a good soul.
She must have been raised well.
Even when she helps us,
There's times when she feels
 hell.

Heather oh kind Heather
Wants to help the world.
We both practice loving folks.
For earth our love's unfurled.

She puts me on the road again,
When I have gone astray.
Many, many desperate times,
She helped me on my way.

Many times I've trusted her,
While trusting no one near.
Many days we'd sit awhile
Creating bits of cheer.

Patricia A Fisher

I love the times I make her
laugh
Cause she might not laugh
much.
She helps so many people.
She helps them stay in touch

With a little bit happier heart
Or an answer for the day.
She asks us all good questions
So we know what to say.

Heather made it possible
For me to get an award
For helping all those people
With books they couldn't afford.

Heather loves her clients.
In this she puts her all.
Most the time I trust her.
We have a similar call.

Since we have a calling,
It's something we must do.
A calling is God's message.
He calls for me and you.

I am so glad I met you.
You're good right to the bone.
Thank you, thank you, thank you.
I rarely feel alone…

P. S. Heather I'm in trouble.
I don't know where to go.
I'm doing the impossible.
The devil is my foe.

These people are the devil.
They hurt me very bad.
You can't help me either.
I am so very sad…

Patricia A Fisher

This day today was much like
hell.
I don't know what they want.
They keep on badly hurting me.
My face is strained and gaunt.

If you have an idea,
Tell me of it now.
I must stop this madness,
And the furrow in my brow.

Help me stop the demons
Who live inside my head.
Please just let me live again,
So I won't end up dead...

On a little bit better day
she would say:

Don't fight it!

It just makes it worse!

Say, "This is what's
happening now. I wish
it was different, but it
isn't."

Go with it!

Heather

Mom, Dennis and I were at a restaurant laughing and having fun. We were a little noisy.

Then one of us said, "What if they make us leave?"

That's when mom said, "Oh well, I've been thrown out of better places than this!"

We about died laughing…

A Life Bigger Than My Illness
(Idea from Ron Markovich L.C.S.W.)

One night, I was going off to sleep, and symptoms of my illness began to appear.

At first I was afraid. Then I told myself that those symptoms were only a small part of my existence. At that moment, I knew that my life was bigger than the fear and rage building inside me.

I thought of the Love, Truth, and Respect I've been receiving for about 40 years, and how I am giving it back.

Patricia A Fisher

That night I thought of my home and loved ones. Instead of being consumed by those symptoms, all the other parts of my life came into view.

My symptoms seemed to be rather small compared to the hugeness of life.

That night I smiled at all my good fortune and all the help I've been given.

That night I realized I was living a better life. There in the dark, I could see clearly how I am living A Life Bigger Than My Illness.

Just Do

What Has

To Be Done

And Get It

Over With!

D. Stanley

Check It Out

Don't Give Your Power Away...

About a week ago I gave a book I wrote to some very important people in my life. The week seemed like a month, as they did not immediately tell me what they thought about it.

My days were very stressful as I waited. Things I previously loved meant less to me. I thought these people were not telling me what they thought, because they decided to put stigma on me.

I was not of a mind to know what to do about my discomfort.

So each day passed with all kinds of thoughts going through my head.

I thought my 'friends' no longer cared about me, or respected me. I felt I could not come to see them anymore. I just knew our friendly connections had been severed, and that we would never see them again.

All these thoughts were of my giving my power away. I depended on their acceptance and approval of my work. I thought they no longer cared about me...

Finally, Dennis asked me, "Why don't you Check it Out?"

I immediately went to them, and asked what they thought about my book.

They both said I did a real good job, and that my writing would help people *with those kinds of problems.*

I disagreed about only people with mental illness getting help from my books. Everyone is affected, and therefore, everyone can benefit.

Yet, I was so relieved! The things that use to give me joy were no longer held in bondage. I could breathe deeply again...

Later, I thought about how I gave my power away. Before I checked it out, my life was lacking the luster it previously had, and I was very unhappy.

I couldn't have let more time go by without knowing how they felt. So I checked it out and almost immediately got my power back.

My whole existence relaxed, and I could enjoy life again.

I don't think a person should hold another in higher regard than themselves, but I think it is common for a person to want the respect of others.

Laura

Here is where I want to introduce my therapist, Laura.

She has an awareness of many potential problems I might be developing, and she is always ready to chuckle at the irony of life.

On her serious side, she is hopeful. On her lighter side she is mischievous.

We have relearned helpful things from each other right from the start (things like equality, kindness, and staying in the moment).

Laura, thank you for sharing your knowledge, and uniqueness with me. I'm honored to welcome you into my life…

With love, respect, truth, and a healthy dose of laughter,

Pat

You Don't Do It As Often As You Use To

My Dennis came home from fishing with a neighbor. I was lying in bed crying, and thinking of ways to kill myself. (Yes this is still happening)...

He was tired, but he put all his problems aside for the hundredth time. We talked and again I am ready to face the world.

When he helps me like that, I get somewhat ambivalent, because he keeps me here when I want to go...

I told 'my' Dennis that he really
must love me, to go through all
these hardships with me.

He said, "You don't do it as often
as you use to."

I smiled because it was true.
Doing therapy, talking with
Dennis, taking my medication,
and writing to the world, has
helped me immensely!

'My' Dennis and I love each other
very much, and we show it to
each other often. Neither of us
takes advantage of the other.

While talking through my tears to
Dennis, I realized I had been
letting people take my power
again.

I was slowly being weakened by people who felt good about staying in control.

My talk and tears with Dennis, make me aware of these things, and I feel like living again. I now feel that I can be around control freaks, and still find my way.

I thank you, dear reader, for reading my books, and for letting me share. I hope my ideas are of some support in your busy, day-to-day lives.

God bless all of you, 'my' Dennis and me, and God bless even the control freaks. Like all of us, they are amazing, but still only human...

A Royal Pain in the Ass

Compulsive behavior has somewhat run my life since adolescence. When I ate, I ate a lot. When I began to drink alcohol, I never measured the amount. I smoked cigarettes a lot for three or four years, then was forced to quit by people who were in control of me (at least I thought so at the time).

These were the years of "free love", so this gave me an excuse to experiment with sex. Back then, drugs were also a big deal, so, of course I had to get in on that too.

Thankfully, I was forced to come back to Denver. Living in Manhattan was where a person could 'get lost' easily, and eventually, I did. It could have been worse as I remember. New York could either make you or break you.

When I got back to Denver, I was still drinking, but had stopped smoking around that time.

Twenty years later, I was driving under the influence, and was stopped by a policeman! I never felt so helpless as when I was sitting in the back seat of a cop car with my hands cuffed behind me...
(I wouldn't advise it!)

On Christmas day of the same year, 1991, I quit drinking. My Dennis and I were at some friends of ours, where I drank a wine cooler. If you ever want to stop drinking, just have a wine cooler. It was all I needed to quit.

What helped me stay away from alcohol, was when I would brag to Dennis, "Dennis, guess what I did without a drink in my hand!" He would congratulate me every time. It became fun, and I became very proud of my accomplishments.

It has been forty years since I stopped smoking, and twenty since I quit drinking.

It seems like now, I could come to grips with eating so much sugar, here at the beginning of another twenty year period.

Well, I still take a sip of Dennis' wine, or have an alcohol free beer. I swear I can feel the one half percent alcohol in an alcohol free beer. It is so strange!

For some people, a sip of wine or a bottle of non-alcohol beer, would make them start abusing alcohol again. (Actually it is alcohol abusing them!)

I pray for everybody we know, and everybody we don't know. So, this means I pray for the recovering alcoholic. Maybe they could pray for my lack of control around sugar.

I know that too much sugar abuses *my* body, and I must control my sugar intake to save my life…

Compulsive behavior will probably not end my life very soon, but it will more than likely stay 'A Royal Pain In The Ass'!

Ya know? I am surprised to have made it to age sixty two. Stopping compulsions like cigarettes and alcohol, most likely gave me more years of walking on this planet.

I live in gratitude that I have come this far, and I live in hope, that I can give up one more compulsion.

They say, "You can never

have too much sugar!"

Who's they?

They are whoever always

says

those important things…

Sometimes

I Allow Myself

To Be

Disappointed

Not Angry...

Patricia A Fisher

For The Love Of Jamie

In the middle of hell
and nowhere to go
I went for 'The Love of Jamie'.

In every moment
in the middle of hell
she was there
with a kind "How are you"?

Then she would listen.
Then she'd be silent.
Then most times
she'd make me laugh.

She'd make me laugh
through the most bitter of tears.
Then she would wander off to
make another person feel better
than how she found them.

What will you see when you look
at the person who is Jamie?

This is difficult, because, how can
you define a mischievous,
mysterious angel?

She is a sweet, funny, noisy spirit
peeking out from under her gray
knit stocking cap.

How do I see Jamie?
She's my friend…

Don't say
That negative thing.

Your brain will hear you
and make it come true.

What is it worth, if you
have to ask for it?

It must be
Worth asking for.

I've heard crazy is doing the same thing over and over again, and expecting a different outcome.

Personally, I think they do it because there is always hope.

Don't

Should

On

Me

Patricia A Fisher

Family Night Speech
At ACMHC

I, Patricia A. Fisher, have experienced the crippling affects of paranoia and isolation. Yet I have built a meaningful and supportive connection with other people. I utilize skills learned in therapy, building a life of Love, Truth, and Respect. I enjoy a wonderful sense of humor, as I actively and deeply "Live a Life Bigger Than My Illness."

I want to thank my therapist of 10 years, Heather Gowin

Laura Rossmassler, MA, my challenging therapist.

My psychiatrist, Anne O. Garrette-Mills, MD.

Randy Stith, for giving me his name as a reference.

Ron Markovich, for giving us his idea about 'living a life bigger than our illnesses.'

All the warriors who fight for their life and respect every single day.

Last but never least, my Dennis for all his love and support I am eternally grateful.

I am honored to be here…

Patricia A Fisher

Tonight, I want to tell you a bit about my journey, as I live a life bigger than my illness. Hopefully this will be of use to you...

I grew up with horrible things happening to me and around me. Sometimes I wonder how I made it this far...

But I don't have to be that person anymore. I no longer have to see the world through resentful eyes. Although there is no cure, I no longer let my illness define who I am, or determine how I live my life. I'm happier than I have ever been.

The following are three rules I choose to live by:

1. I take my medicine just in case it helps me.
2. I do volunteer work, while I practice loving people.
3. I stay very close to my higher power.

(1.) My first rule, taking my medicine, is definitely a challenge. It is so much of a challenge I wrote a piece about it called 'Just In Case'. I'd like to read it to you now.

Patricia A Fisher

Just In Case

Just in case
My meds work,

I take them
Every day.

"Just in case
They help me,"

Is what
I always say.

They may just
Solve my problems

With what comes
To my mind.

My doctors
Always ask me,

When I am
In a bind,

"Do you take
Your meds dear,

Because we see
Your pain?"

"It helps you
Think more clearly,

When it gets to
Your brain".

I tell them
"Yes I take it,

Just in case
It works.

It may just help
That part of me-

That part of me
That hurts."

My mental health
Professionals

Are totally
Surprised!

I do
What they tell me.

They are so
Very wise

I'm told to trust
Professionals

Hired
For my health.

I feel they're
More important

Than monetary
Wealth.

I just cannot
Do everything

The doctors
Say to me.

Yes, it seems
Impossible,

Though I pay
A fee.

Patricia A Fisher

So, I do
Everything I can

To try
And get along.

I just do
The best I can.

Now how can that
Be wrong?

The taking of
My medicine

Is where
I stay more true.

Just in case
It helps me

It's something
I can do.

(2.) My second rule, doing volunteer work, is where I practice loving people.

Many years ago I was told, "Volunteer! Volunteer! It's helpful to have structure". So I would go out and do work that just didn't seem meaningful. I would count the minutes until I could leave the building. Then I would go home and lay under the covers.

My life felt empty... I thought volunteer work was not for me.

Then, I started to practice loving people. I discovered that when my heart was engaged, even "menial" jobs became a lot easier.

My job became both enjoyable
and meaningful-even when
cleaning bathrooms!

What also helped was working
side by side with my husband.
So having a buddy to work with
makes a big difference!

We find ourselves doing for others
what we would want done for us.

I have stopped counting minutes.
In fact, we find ourselves working
more hours than what we are
asked to do!

I now enjoy living a life of service.

It has been fun to give gifts, but volunteer work means a person gives of his or her self. I get to feel my body moving as I use my muscles. Plus, I get endorphins. These are little hormones that are activated when a person exercises. They can make a person feel real good, and they're free.

A sense of belonging comes as a bonus, and I feel so good about contributing to our world.

(3.) My third rule is being grateful to a higher power.

I've written and published 12 books. All that writing may have helped me find myself. It may have helped me find my higher power.

For a long time, I begged my higher power for what I wanted. The answers never seemed to come. Finally, I started saying thanks for what I already had...

I started getting answers...

While carrying toilet paper to a restroom, this feeling came over me. I started saying, "Thank you God! Thank you for this moment."

I looked down at my hands holding the TP, And I laughed to myself. I felt so happy to be alive! On this beautiful summer day there was peace in my heart.

Well folks, I take my meds, which is now part of a mission I'm on to feel good. I make sure my med trays are filled every 2 weeks, and I make sure I take them every day.

Doing volunteer work just makes me happy. It gives me a feeling of belonging, and it boosts my self esteem.

Being grateful to a higher power, for what I already have, fills my heart to overflowing, and I am never alone.

Since I embraced all these things, I am living a life bigger than my illness. I am no longer trapped within the walls of paranoia, depression, and loneliness.

If I were to give you a huge gift tonight, it would be that you too could live a life bigger than your fear, bigger than your depression, bigger than your anger. I would give to you a life bigger than your illness...

WITH LOVE, TRUTH, RESPECT, AND LAUGHTER,

I THANK YOU...

Patricia A. Fisher

The Absence of Awful

Patricia A Fisher

My Dennis

And Me

And Puppy

Makes three

Now A Complete

Family

Patricia A Fisher

Lately I am finding that I write less about illness. This only tells me that I am living a life bigger than my illness.

I hope you are not bored by my stories about Dennis and our love for each other. I just want to show you that a long, loving marriage is possible to obtain and still a worthwhile endeavor.

Mental illness does not have to prevent a meaningful connection with another person. If Dennis and I can do it, maybe you can too.

I wish you love and laughter, and may all your good dreams come true.

The Absence of Awful

Many, many years ago
Invisible was I.

Born a lonely munchkin,
Who'd later want to die.

I almost died a lot of times.
I'd waste my life away.

Fun and games were hardly
there.
I couldn't face the day!

There's good and bad in
humanity.
Sometimes we really hurt!

Depression takes its' toll here.
Six foot under dirt!

Rage is part of the problem.
It can't be any good,

For the person raging,
Or the person who never would.

I've reached the bottom
A million times.
What hell it was for me.

My Dennis stood there
By my side.
How helpless there was he.

He witnessed all my torture.
He blessed me with his love.

He seemed to be connected
To our Heavenly Father above…

He does these things
Around the house,
And never tells me so.

Every time I find one,
My heart gets all aglow.

I go to him to celebrate
Surprises that he's done.

He says, "You celebrate
everything!"
Yes, sometimes we have fun.

He walks the walk,
And talks the talk.
His actions say it all.

He proves to me
He's good, you see.
My Dennis walks so tall!

Now, awful things can happen,
But there's a lot of good.

(The loving of each other-
More than you think you could.)

The love in your heart
Will come along.
I promise this to be.

Love is, 'The Absence of Awful'.
It seems this way to me…

My Dennis and I were taking a trip to Glenwood Springs, Colorado.

Dennis asked mom, "Connie, would like to go to Glenwood with us?"

She said, "No, I don't feel very well."

Dennis said, "Would you rather feel not very well at Glenwood, or not feel very well at home?"

The three of us had a wonderful trip!

Nickolas

Our best friends, many years ago,
had two children. One of
them was Nickolas.

One night I babysat him. He was
a brand new infant.

Not having experience with
babysitting, I put him on his
tummy next to me on the couch.
I proceeded to watch him breathe
for approximately two
hours.

Somewhere, during this time, I
put his tiny foot in my mouth. I
don't know why. It was just so
cute.

Patricia A Fisher

Many years later, Nick grew into a handsome, six foot four, kind young man.

I tease him about my putting his little foot in my mouth.

He says, "I bet you can't do that now."

I say, "No because I'm too busy putting my own foot in my mouth."

A Blue Balloon

One day, a long time ago, we were to meet some friends at Washington Park in Denver. Mayor Peña was running for office, and there was a big rally going on.

Our friends told us to look for a blue balloon, because there would be a huge crowd, and we would be able to find them easier…

When we got to the park, we couldn't believe our eyes! We saw blue balloons as far as the eye could see! There were thousands of them!

Patricia A Fisher

It appears Peña supporters were giving out blue balloons that day.

After much searching, we finally found our friends.

We still laugh at that day...

Night-night My Sweet Darlin'

Night-night my sweet darlin'.
I've said it all before.

Lots of years with you –
Maybe a little more.

People just don't stay
Married to each other.

They break up very quickly,
So they can find another.

A throwaway society,
Nothing's sacred now.

Not words from our weddings,
Where we have made a vow.

Patricia A Fisher

No special pen or pencil.
No refill when used up.

We throw them out when empty,
And do not interrupt,

The pace of hurry hurry,
Of running here and there.

We must be on our guard.
There's no time left to care.

To care
About somebody

Who's there
Through thick and thin.

There won't be time
To love them –

No time
For you and him...

So we throw away
Our marriage.

Like we did
That pen,

And get another
Partner,

And do it all
Again…

I cannot see
The sense

Of all this
Going on.

You turn 'round
For a minute.

The one you loved
Is gone!

Patricia A Fisher

Who is this
New person

Walking
By your side?

Why do you not
Know them?

Is this
Because of pride?

So, night-night
My sweet darlin'.

Together all
These years.

We have been
Together

Through laughter
And through tears

Night-night
My true love

I'll not
Throw you away.

Our vows from our
Wedding

Mean I'm here
To stay.

The secret of
Longevity –

Being married
Long,

Is that we both
Stay married.

Each of us
Belong.

Patricia A Fisher

We share our lives
In support

Of what
The other needs.

We show love
To each other

By doing
Little deeds.

We are taking
Lots of years

To say,
"I love you, dear."

Through thick and thin
Together,

We will be
Right here.

We're taking
All our lifetime

To say,
"I know you well."

For years
Of almost Forty

Nothing broke
The spell.

So, night-night
My sweet darlin'.

For I am
Giving you,

The promise
Of forever.

Forever
I'll be true…

Patricia A Fisher

October's Money

Figure out to the day

Money we must pay.

Oh! What can I say?

We're broke...

What can we two do

Just to get us through?

I'll stay close to you.

We'll be safe...

Our stocks keep going down,

But we don't wear a frown.

How does all this sound?

Ridiculous…

'Cause money pays for toys,

For older girls and boys,

I think of all my joys,

And I smile…

Patricia A Fisher

Half way through September,

I suddenly remember,

Like a dying ember,

We've spent October's money...

But he and I live on,

Though our money's gone.

The truth begins to dawn.

There is hope...

Out by Noon on Saturday

Due to our stocks going down, we had to lower our income by one third. Hence, we could no longer financially support our home, and travel too. So, our home is being put on the market.

Both Dennis and I have shed many tears. For we have lived here almost twenty seven years. It's with a sweet sadness that we leave our beautiful home.

We can still support our Jeep Liberty, and a 30 foot motor home. Thank God they are both paid for, and still pretty new.

So, we have decided to put into storage all our furniture we want to keep. Then, we'll go on the road until we need assisted living or something.

We're going to pack what we can into both the motor home and our little red Jeep. We'll hitch the Jeep to the back of that motor home. This will just be another adventure. The only difference is, we won't have our house to come home to…

When I think of all this modification of belongings, I still feel fortunate. I still have 'my' Dennis, and, of course, that is most important.

Our RV will be our only home.
At least this is the plan…

You would think that our entry
into senior citizenship would be
more secure. It would seem as if
we would be living peacefully in
our home of twenty seven years.

Yet, soon we will be uprooted,
and on the road to who knows
where! There may be many
people who would like this kind of
freedom…

Little by little, I am getting away
from the tears, and I am moving
on. We will indeed be going on
another adventure! This
adventure will just last longer
than any we have enjoyed.

Somehow we have managed to have good health insurance. This is another fortunate thing.

So, you see, we still have our toys, and we have pretty good health. We have each other, and that is huge!

With all these wonderful gifts, we will be ready. We'll be ready for that day, when we are politely asked, "Will you be 'Out by Noon on Saturday?"

LATER

My Dennis and I changed our minds about selling our precious home.

After meeting with our realtor, we became discouraged, but we were very appreciative of our home in many ways. So, we decided to keep it.

We decided that if we wanted to help ourselves financially, we would need to work for our camping space everywhere we went. We could not own our home and travel as well. That was for sure!

Patricia A Fisher

We both had a lot of apprehension, because neither of us has worked for someone else for many years. I also thought that I would not be hired because of my illness.

Yet, we applied for work at a couple of campgrounds out of state.

Sure enough, without much delay, one of those state campgrounds gave us the job!

I am still ecstatic! I was chosen without stigma attached. How fun it is to be treated like an almost normal person (whatever that is)!

We leave in a week, and I am ready now!

When one door closes, another door opens. I guess we just have to keep our eyes open to see it.

Money will still be scarce, but we will stay vigilant, as we continually look for ways to support our home and our traveling.

I am so ready for this trip, as it will be yet another adventure for 'my' sweet Dennis and me!

MUCH LATER:

Finally, we have made a very important decision! We are selling our beautiful home and we are going on the road permanently!

My Dennis was having one of his awful pressure headaches.

He said, "I'm having so much pain my head could explode!"

I said, "If your head explodes, there will be thoughts everywhere!"

A Thorn Must Be Removed Before Healing Can Begin

We've probably all heard the story about a mouse removing a large thorn from the gigantic paw of a lion.

They became great friends, and, I believe, the lion eventually returned the favor to the mouse.

As we people live our lives, our thorns may be a little different, but the rule is still the same.

My particular thorn was caused by our asking for an application to work here at our special camping place.

I was beginning to have extremely strong symptoms, and they were beginning to show. Then, Dennis asked me, "Are you afraid to work here?"

Instantly, it hit home with me! This was the reason for that painful thorn in my 'paw'.

I feared having symptoms, and then losing my job. It would affect 'my' Dennis as well, and then we might never be welcome here again…

Then it was gone… Now, I can feel my energy coming back.

With help from 'my' Dennis, my health professionals, and my own warrior like tendencies, I won another inner battle.

Now this fear is gone, and that thorn is no longer there. For my Dennis did not find the right answer. He found the right question, and this removed the thorn.

Like the lion and the mouse, I walk by the side of 'my' Dennis. At times, I have needed to remove a thorn from *his* 'paw'…

This is a part of our friendship and marriage. This is a part of our love. For every once in awhile, we each have a thorn that must be removed before healing can begin…

Have you ever heard

about the stupid guy

who snorted the

wrong coke

and drown?

yuk-yuk-yuk

My Dennis and Me

I'll start this life time story
Between the two of us
Our marriage is forever
I have things to discuss

About how you
Would hold me.
You'd whisper
In my ear,

And tell me
Everything
To make me smile.

You'd keep the world
From entering
Our private
Rendezvous.

We'd dream and talk
And be
Just for awhile.

I've always been
Amazed by you,
Your truth
So overflowing.

My faith in what
You'd say
Was so complete.

You've never been
Judgmental.
You equaled every man
Never any trace of real conceit.

You now must know
I love you.
You now must stay
In sight.

I love you
Even more
My dear
I cry.

For we have
Been together
Through times
That weren't so good.

We've earned the right
To never say goodbye.

Patricia A Fisher

So, be with me
My darling
Though the sun
Is setting

And silver gray is showing
In our hair.

We've come too far
To stop now-
To cut the ties
That bind.

We have a lot
More moments
We can share.

So, though our years
Turn golden,
Our bones begin
To creak

Our bodies
Are not like
They use to be.

I'm glad
I met you darling.
The years
Have not been bad.

So come my love
And sit right here with me.

Patricia A Fisher

Our
Sweet
Kris

Kris Kringle

We were just
My Dennis and me.
We were living
Alone you see.

Days went by
We had some fun
We'd say goodnight
When day was done.

I started thinking,
How can this be?
I'd like to start
A family.

I tell my Dennis
A lot of times.
I want a fam'.
(So here's these rhymes)

Patricia A Fisher

Dennis, Dennis
Do you fear?
I want to start
A family here.

He said to me.
"My dearest wife
Go ahead.
Go live your life."

It went that way
Almost a year.
Every talk
He made it clear.

You've gotta be joking.
You've got to see.
I'm your only
Family,

Then one day
We got a pup.
Since that time
Our hearts filled up

With all our love
For this young pet.
The three of us
Just went in debt.

Shots and checkups
And grooming too,
Nothing stopped us
From loving you.

He weighs five pounds.
We call him her!
He's a little
Ball of fur.

Patricia A Fisher

The vet would also
Call him her.
It was funny,
And did occur.

We're training Kris.
It's easy to do.
He learns so fast.
Intelligent too.

He loves the snow.
I cannot say
How cute he was
That snowy day!

He loved to eat
The fallen snow.
What it was
He didn't know.

For he would take
A flying leap,
And disappear…
The snow was deep!

We'd see him jump
And dance around,
And chase the snow flakes
That he found.

He'd be so excited
'Cause never did he
Know what this stuff
So white could be.

He sure had a ball!
All crazy he was.
He was this tiny
Ball of fuzz.

Patricia A Fisher

For he had snow
All over his fur,
And most on his face,
'Twas funny I'm sure.

What wonderful fun
For Dennis and me
'Cause now all of us
Are a family of three.

When morning is here,
He jumps on the sheets.
He gives us both kisses
Without having treats.

Every morning
Exciting is he.
So glad to see us,
And so full of glee!

If you are sad,
It never will last.
He goes for your face
Incredibly fast!

He licks you and licks you.
You open your eyes.
So very much joy
For his little size.

So many times
He does something new
'Cause he's just a pup.
What else can he do?

He's five months of age.
Has seven months more.
He'll be one year old.
Such fun is in store.

Patricia A Fisher

Fun Christmas day-
The day of his birth.
Little Kris Kringle
What is he worth?

We now have Christmas
Every day.
What's wrong with that?
That's what I say.

Christmas all year,
How happy are we,
A proud little family
A family of three...

Chipmunk Food

We were camping in the Rocky Mountains. My toe nails were painted red.

This little chipmunk scampered over, and tried to bite my toe off!

Evidently he thought my toe nails were some kind of chipmunk food.

Patricia A Fisher

My side of the Family

The challenge of a Lifetime…

Patricia A Fisher

ITSMEEE

Afraid and abandon
When I was young
Caused me to do the same

To the people I love
And care about.
I'm not searching for whom
To blame.

How can I remotely
Discuss this now,
When I don't even know
What's real?

"Feelings aren't facts"
They said in my group
So I cannot believe
What I feel!

Patricia A Fisher

When I get close
And start to care
"Bout a friend
Or family,

I cannot depend
On either of them.
Maybe they
Can't depend on me!

If the "big secret"
Is where I hide,
Oh, yes,
I think it could be.

Maybe it isn't
They who change.
Could be
That 'ITSMEEE'...

Patricia A Fisher

It's No Longer Christmas

If it was Christmas
We sisters would be
All kinds of loving
Toward each of us three.

We'd not turn away
When one wants to call.
So happy we'd be
Good wishes and all.

We would give gifts
And open our heart.
Nothing on earth
Could keep us apart.

How I love Christmas,
And ways that we change.
We're so warm and loving,
I'd not rearrange,

The warmness
Of Christmas
Our hearts
All aglow.

We come
A bit closer
The fear
Starts to go.

Then Christmas
Is over
We each
Go our way.

Old feelings
Of fear
Won't keep us
At bay.

Patricia A Fisher

Crippled
By fear
Is how
We all were

Our hearts
Have stopped breaking
I hope it's
For sure

This has all
Happened
To their hearts
And mine.

Our hearts
Have broken
Many
A time...

Now we
Won't let them.
Our hearts
Cannot break!

We will
No longer
Feel our hearts
Ache.

For we so
Want sisters
Loving
And true

All through
The year.
So what
Can we do?

Patricia A Fisher

What of our hearts
Hurting us three
Wanting that love
'Tween sisters you see?

Can we all take it –
These feelings are blind
One minute happy
Then we change our mind

With all of these changes
It's good that we see
It's no Longer Christmas
But love can still be...

Sixteen of Me

Why can't my fam'
Be more like me?

They'd understand,
And maybe they'd see,

How I am right
Just all of the time,

And things that I do
Are never a crime!

They'd finally see
My point of view,

How great I am,
And beautiful too!

They'd be very bright,
Exactly like me!

They'd want to be near.
What fun it would be!

They would keep saying,
You have a smart brain.

I am amazed
At your fortune and fame!

They would so love
The way that I am!

'Sixteen of me'
Would be my whole fam'!

We're Only Human

Many families, of people with mental illnesses, would give everything they own to see their loved ones again. A lot of times, these families would be happy to just lay eyes on these afflicted family members.

Many times, members of my family seemed to push me away. They would seem scared of getting to close, not only to me but with other family members.

Out in the world I have met so many people who care about me. We laugh together, and exchange our life experiences.

From them, I get respect, and they warm my heart.

One time, a part of my family had an upset, and we all went our own ways for long while.

I remember receiving an "I can't be around family" letter.

Meanwhile, 'my' Dennis and I are camped in one of New Mexico's beautiful and peaceful deserts.

Already, we have enjoyed a new friendship. We have fun with this couple we have only just met. I find myself comparing them to parts of my own family, and I am saddened.

Maybe I am misguided as to how close family is suppose to be…

All my life I have waited for things to get better and for us to get closer. I used to blame myself when we didn't.

At times, it seems, we'll be ok, and we are closer. Then we get that old insecurity. I try to accept my part of the responsibility and try not to blame anyone.

Why can't we all just be a close family. It's a waste of time to stay so separate for so long. The sooner people are forgiven, the sooner the laughter and love can begin again. We're only human, and we're going to make mistakes!

Patricia A Fisher

Daily

Maintenance

Is

A Full Time Job

Patricia A Fisher

Go Back to Basics

I finally made a list of all I need to do just to maintain my life – the bare necessities of my daily existence. I think that's why people retire.

1.They need all that extra time to take all the pills.

2. And in my case, do all the blood tests.

3. They need plenty of time to swallow the fiber.

4. And get life preserving exercise.

5. Then there's taking a shower.

6. For some, putting on make-up.

7. They have to eat right.

8. And drink plenty of water.

9. Brush their teeth.

10. Comb their hair.

11. Find some clothes to wear.

12. With this done go out and greet the day with a smile.

Actually all ages need a list like this, but at older ages, it becomes an absolute necessity.

My own list seems to get longer and longer. There is a mind-boggling number of helpful things I have written down.

With this writing, I hope I can help my readers *and* myself. Maybe this account, of maintaining my own life, will help some of you to not feel so alone in *your* efforts. I know I feel better already.

I'm finding that, though a bit frustrating, this list helps me enjoy life.

It's like a foundation. It appears that a person must do all these things, and then start building from there.

Maybe I never learned to actually do thorough, basic maintenance. Because of this, it is oh so important now!

Life isn't all lists and rules. Life can have laughter and meaning. Yet, it's like my Dad use to say, "When all else fails, Go Back to Basics."

Patricia A Fisher

I like raw vegetables

Better

When I'm not on a

Diet.

Patricia A Fisher

Stories

of

Camp Hosting

Featuring

Linda's Song

Patricia A Fisher

My Dear Readers,

As you may remember from my previous books, I have been told that they have helped many people. I help them by sharing most of my secrets in support of mental wellness.

Sharing these secrets with some of the people at places Dennis and I volunteer, makes me wonder if they will understand. They may not rehire us and this particular work is a win-win situation. We work in turn for what we need and they get help from what we do. Plus, we have found much joy and sense of belonging as we practice loving the people we meet.

Introduction to Peaceful:

We are both honored and privileged to be here, working and chatting with others.

If Pat is 'patched up' and otherwise well again, we hope to be welcome back next season.

You really have a beautiful place here. We've lived in this area for years, and just never came up to work or play.

Here's a piece I wrote about Golden Gate Canyon State Park.

Love, and Good wishes,
Pat and Dennis

A Place Called Peaceful
(Golden Gate Canyon State Park)

There is a place
Called Peaceful,
If only
In my mind.

It's beauty
Is delicious.
It's people
Are so kind.

Believe me
When I say this.
The altitude
Is high

Just about
9000 feet
So great
For birds to fly.

Patricia A Fisher

Right here
We spent the summer.
We had
Our ups and downs,

But Mostly
We were happy.
Rarely we had frowns.

The pines are tall
In peaceful
All such
Lovely green.

The ground is
Perfectly covered.
The air is
Fresh and clean.

These are the
Rocky Mountains
With cliffs
And bubbling streams.

This is so close
To the place of my birth
Now a part
Of my dreams.

I invite you now
To peaceful.
Otherwise
You won't know

The feel of cool
Summer breezes
Or the gift
Of new fallen snow.

Patricia A Fisher

The magic
Of mother nature,
Our earth's what
She can adorn.

She's in this dream
I have in my heart
Ever since
I was born...

Why Must We Have War

The Colorado mountains
Were home so long ago.
The jagged cliffs
And rocks and trees
Remind me I should go.

As a little tiny girl,
I loved the mountains so.
It's been many, many, years.
The roaring wind would blow.

Up into the tops of pines
Exciting me a lot
They'd do a dance
Sway back and forth
When I was just a tot.

Patricia A Fisher

Once there was a flimsy tree
A small one that we found.
My sister climbed up to the top
Without her falling down.

She smiled and giggled
Back and forth.
The tree just wouldn't break.
Other memories I have had
Like photos that you take.

Once we saw a marmot.
It had a funny bark.
Just a fluffy ball of fur
On top of this great park.

Timber creek is barren now.
How mournfully I cry…
All those trees had beetle kill.
Mother Nature made them die.

Fifty five years later
I'm "Rocky Mountain High".
These could be the same trees
Beneath that clear blue sky.

Up here in these mountains
Made by God above
The trees are now in trouble,
The same trees that I love.

It seems 'my' trees are dying.
The beetles think they're food.
They eat the trees beneath their
bark.
I thought this would improve.

People started cutting down
The beautiful Lodge Pole Pines.
They turned red from beetle kill.
And you can see the signs.

Riding through the Rockies,
When there it was, a crime,
A pile of dead old pine trees
I thought that I was fine,

Until I saw the trees I loved
Dead and piled up.
It seemed just like a burial
ground,
Which made my eyes well up.

I can't explain
Just how I felt
Passing by this scene.
The beautiful trees
That I had known
Magnificent, lovely green,

They were changed to red rot
No signs of lovely green
Just put there in a pile
Like they didn't mean a thing.

Nature has a
Way to prune
The trees
And all that grows.

Fire from the
Lightning
As everybody knows

Lightning causes fires.
Animals run away.
Fires that burn
The trees and brush
Make birds fly on that day.

When the green
Starts coming back,
The animals will eat
Varieties of plants and all.
They think it is a treat.

Patricia A Fisher

The forest goes through changes
All the living things
Little trees start growing back.
That's when my heart sings!

So, back there in my childhood
Remembering my smile,
My little sister on that tree
Rocking for awhile.

Maybe that small and flimsy tree
That's back within my mind
Was one big tree that made it
through.
That's what I'd like to find.

I try to think of beetles
That really change the trees
They need food for living
As all the birds and bees…

Standing with some people
Trying to say what's right.
    Beetles are of nature. But
trees don't like to fight.

So I said, "What's happening".
I asked them, "What's the fuss?.
For the first time in my life I said
"War is there for us".

So we must spray our poison
On our lovely trees
A little war of beetle kill
For problems such as these

This is such a little war
'Tween beetles and the trees.
We stepped in to help trees win
And hear them in the breeze.

Patricia A Fisher

For the first time in my life
I understood, "What for?"
I understood, "The reason
Why our earth needs war".

Protecting any beauty
That we have on this earth
War is what must happen
For that is what it's worth...

What Am I?

(Questions and answers for the kids at
Golden Gate Canyon State Park in
Colorado)

These small and pretty carnivore
Live in a very odd home

They travel up and down the hills
They're not a bird to roam

Their moms and dads are
teachers
For their baby chicks

The babies copy mom and dad
And learn all of their tricks.

Patricia A Fisher

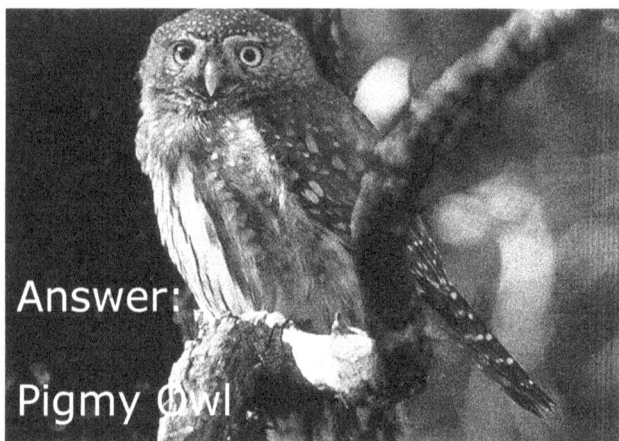

Answer:

Pigmy Owl

What Am I?

This flower is a treasure
In different shades of blue

Petals look like little horns
It is a state flower too.

Butterflies and long tailed moths
And little hummingbirds

Love their yummy nectar
You can name them in three
words.

Patricia A Fisher

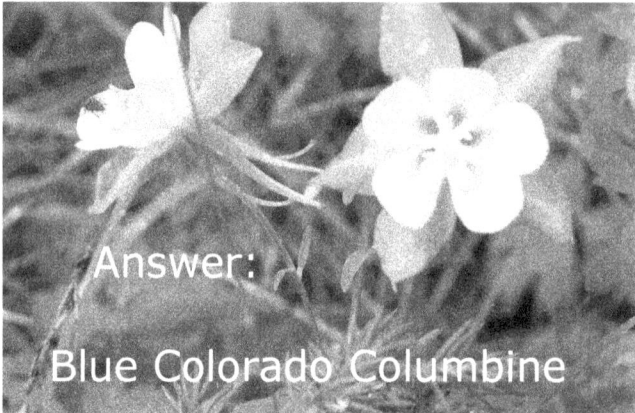

Answer:

Blue Colorado Columbine

What Am I?

A Large and furry animal
Came to the park today.

It came to eat the goodies
From the dumpster that fine day.

But the rangers saw it coming.
The dumpster lid was braced.

The animal tried to pry it loose
So it could have a taste.

After lots of trying
The animal mad that day

Stood on top the dumpster
Did his business and walked
away…

(A True Story

Patricia A Fisher

Answer:
Black Bear

The Absence of Awful

Patricia A Fisher

What Am I?

These mammals are big,
And they can be seen,
Out in the crop fields,
In cool early spring.

The best time to see them
Is at dusk or dawn,
For they are most active,
When sunlight is gone.

They look kind of scruffy
When winter is through.
The male ones grow antlers
When summer is due.

Look at the herds,
Where they find their food.
Mostly in summer
They bear all their brood.

You'll see little fawns
Most hidden away.
Their mommas look on
In grass where they lay.

Patricia A Fisher

Answer:

Mule Deer

The Absence of Awful

Patricia A Fisher

What Am I?

They raise their tail when
running,
They're smaller than cousins that
be.

They eat from a dense vegetation
Which makes them so hard to
see.

They wander among the
cottonwoods,
The willows and alders you'll see,

Lining streams and river beds.
Find pathways to waters that be.

For on these pathways to water,
The animals will come to feed.

They have no reason to migrate.
They have everything they need.

For once you find a treasure,
A place with all these things,

You'll see plenty of animals
That Mother Nature brings.

Patricia A Fisher

Answer:
Whitetail Deer

Not Really My Son
Vega State Park

I can't hold my head up.
I'm hurting so bad.

This is the worst week
I've ever had!

I let my poor heart
Be broken in two,

Because I began
To care about you.

You'd come to my door
And stay for awhile.

You won my heart
Smile after smile.

Patricia A Fisher

I felt so maternal
Toward you each day.

I'd smile with my heart,
Just feeling this way.

You were my kid
Or someone as close.

I don't know the day
I loved you the most.

Is this that pain
To parent from child?

When you went away
I no longer smiled.

I laid in my bed
And slept the day through.

I could not get over
This new loss of you.

The Absence of Awful

I knew in my mind
I must let you go.

I felt in my heart
Sad feelings of woe.

Are you like my son
On his first day of school

Learning 'bout math
And that old golden rule?

Are you like my son
Needing some space?

Does this explain
The tears on my face?

What happens now?
What can I do?

Somehow I need
To get over you.

Patricia A Fisher

How can this happen?
Do we disagree?

Did you pretend
To give love to me?

Your smile and your words
Spoken so true,

Brought me to think
This was love from you.

We hugged pretty often
Which felt really good!

And then you were gone.
I did what I could,

To just let you go
Though I am sad.

You were the only
Child that I had.

The Absence of Awful

I know 'twas pretend
That you were the one,

But I really loved you
Like you were my son…

So come back to see us –
That's if you care.

If you really love us,
We will be there.

We'll give to you
Some coffee to drink,

A kind loving word,
What do you think?

If you don't love us
Like you did before,

I guess we won't see you
Around anymore…

Dennis and I were hosting at yet another campground. As we settled in, I found a rule book. In it was a rule that campers could only have 3.2 beer in the park.

So Dennis and I threw out all of our alcohol free beer, and bought 3.2.

(Not really)

Jeff and Lisa
(The children of friends on the road)

Your Dad and Mom
Did love you

Even before
You were here.

You were a sparkle
In their eyes.

Their thoughts of you
Were dear.

And then you grew
In your Mama's womb

So safe, so warm,
So new.

Patricia A Fisher

The only thought
That they had then

Was giving life
To you.

So, later on
You were born

To Mom and Dad's
Delight.

They both could see
Already

That you were
Very bright!

Everything
Was new to you,

Even your
Little toes

Mom and Dad
Took care of you,

And everybody
Knows,

Each new thing
That you would do

Your Mom and Dad
We're proud.

At two years old
You yelled out "no".

In a voice
So very loud!

They have good lungs
Oh, I must say!

They're getting stronger
Every day!

Patricia A Fisher

Age 2, then 4,
A little more

They saw your first step
'Crost the floor.

A tear came down
Your Mama's cheek,

Your Dad so proud
He couldn't speak.

So they just watched
To keep you well.

They walked behind
In case you fell.

A real huge step,
Both Mom and Dad,

Gave it everything
They had.

My dear babes
Please understand.

You both have grown
To someone grand.

Jeff and Lisa
You're both cleaver,

Both of you
Our best endeavor.

You're our kids
Past age 18.

Each our child
Through everything!

If you fail
At what you try,

We'll be close
If you should cry.

Patricia A Fisher

Our love for you
Is never ending.

In this note
It's love we're sending.

You're full grown.
I'll grant you that.

Glad we had
This little chat.

Jeff and Lisa
To you now.

Love forever,
This we vow...

Linda's Song
(Ranger Without A Badge)

Intro to Linda's Song:
Words for intro to Linda's song written by Donald L and Marjorie Smith.
Music to Linda's song by Donald L Smith. Used with permission.

    D
  There's a place in Colorado
         G
  Called Vega Reservoir
    A
Where the deer and bear roam about.
   D
  There's a little brown eyed ranger
         G
  Who works in despair,
   A   *D*
A ranger with no badge.

195

Patricia A Fisher

<u>Words to Linda's Song:</u>
By Pat Fisher
(spoken with background music)

  D
 Crap! Where did my badge go?
      G
  I looked for it last night!
   A
   Was it after dinner?
       D
  Or before I had a bite?

   D
  What will everybody think
        G
 When they hear of my plight?
    A
   I'm just not in uniform
   D
  Without it shining bright!

196

      D
A little piece of metal
              G
That means so much to me.
     A
Crap! Where did my badge go?
     D
My God! Where can it be?

      D
I've searched all over
        everywhere,
             G
And I've looked high and low!

My boss will be so mad at me!
   A   *D*
What if he lets me go?

Patricia A Fisher

_D_
This shiny little metal
                        _G_
Would sit upon my chest
_A_
And make me feel important
                  _D_
So I would do my best.

_D_
But now a tear runs down my
cheek.
            _G_
I'm still a ranger, see…
      _A_   **_D_**
But I'm a ranger with no badge.

(NO MUSIC)

Sad little ranger me…

Finish with cord run **_D G A D_**

198

Was There Ever Really A Camelot?
(Leaving Vega State Park of Colorado
A true story and real people)

My thoughts went back to
Camelot.
Tears welled up in my eyes.
I thought of a wise old wizard
With a heart of gigantic size.

She speaks out loud to the
valley,
"May peace and love abound!"
Their home in the middle of
mountains,
A field lays all around.

There I would walk in magic.
This place just spoke to my
heart.
My soul would sing with
abandon.
Of this valley, I was a part.

Meanwhile, up on the mountain,
A King and Queen reside.
We thought it would last forever,
A place where we could abide…

As dedicated subjects,
Their wish was our command.
Anything for Camelot
Was the rule by which we'd
stand.

I thought there was a table
With all of us around.
All of us were equal.
A magical kingdom we found!

Was there ever really a Camelot?
I thought for sure there was!
Remote and full of good things,
I would smile just because.

Was I the only subject
Who loved the King and Queen,
Who cherished every animal,
And every beautiful scene?

Was I the only believer
That certainly God lived here?
Was I in love with the King and
Queen
And their kingdom without fear?

I loved all of the subjects.
I cried from love of the land.
Were my man and I so
dispensable
That the King so good and
grand,

Would ban us both from the
kingdom?
I will never understand.
Was there ever really a Camelot,
An incredible make believe land

The King stopped loving his
subjects.
He made us go away.
My man and I had sadness
Whenever we thought of that
day.

Instead of helping our problem,
Saying, "Go and you both get
well.
Then come back when you're
ready."
Instead Camelot fell!

Was there ever really a Camelot?
Or was it all in my mind?
Was all of the love a fantasy?
Why were the people unkind?

The wizard of the valley,
And her mate of many years,
Cried for the falling of Camelot,
With a river made of tears.

I still believe in Camelot.
I believe in the King and Queen.
I believe in all of its subjects,
And the wizard now serene.

I believe that Camelot's
sleeping,
And waiting someplace good,
For God to wake it some
morning,
Like I've hoped and prayed that
He would...

Patricia A Fisher

My

Saving

Grace

My

Higher

Power

Patricia A Fisher

I ask people,
"Want to see a miracle?"

They say,
"I guess so"...

So, I show them my
moving index finger.
Most people still don't
understand.

So, I ask them, "Well,
could you make one of
these?"

Patricia A Fisher

Let's hold hands

Until

The love comes

Back.

It's Never Too Late

At times before
I cried a lot –
So many
Broken dreams.

At times before,
When I was young,
My tears came down
In streams.

I wasted time
Just feeling bad,
And wanting
Better days.

I lost my chance
For happiness
In many, many
Ways…

Patricia A Fisher

Later on,
When old I was,
My heart was
Filling up,

With love and joy
And laughter,
As God filled up
My cup!

He gave me truth.
I found myself.
Respect just came
Along.

The best of these
He gave me love.
Now how
Can that be wrong?

It's Never Too Late
For all these things –
Love, respect
And truth.

All the three
Were gifts for me,
My humor
Is the proof.

Now my days
Are filled with joy.
I wake up
Every morn

To find a smile
In my heart.
I'm glad
That I was born.

A Tribute To Our Beloved Patsy Cissell
(We all miss you!)

Patsy, oh sweet Patsy
The joy you brought to us…

You're a warrior
Through and through,
But never mean to us.

At Christmas time
You shined and shined,
Enjoying every bit.

You made those
Odd green dumplings
That really made a hit!

The Absence of Awful

You brought to us
Some candy,
That fudge
That we adored!

Yet, we chose
Your laughter.
It could not be
Ignored.

Laughter was
Your legacy.
You passed it down to us.

We never will
Forget you.
You always were a plus.

Patricia A Fisher

Patsy, we all miss you.
We feel you pass away.

With sadness near
If you were here,
You'd say please laugh and play!

Patsy, you'll find peace
In Heaven way up high.

God has opened up his arms
To hold you if you cry.

For he will see
That you can rest,
And let the bad subside.

I have heard
For times we hurt
God has even cried...

But you won't have
To fight the fight
That you faced every day.

Please let go
Of all your pain
As you go on your way.

If we could wish
One thing for you
While you are up above,

That you'll receive
All that's good,
But most of all pure love.

A Point to Ponder

Lately, I have put a lot of ducks in a row concerning my belief in Christianity.

After talking with my husband and friends, I was finally able to see the sequence of events.

I have always had pieces of information, but just recently, everything came together in my heart, mind and soul.

I never could connect, with why God's sacrifice of his Son, could change the world so much.

Then I realized that, way back in time, people use to sacrifice living things a lot. This was usually done in the name of God. So, sacrifice was a big thing back then.

I had heard of a sacrificial lamb, but never connected the dots till lately.

It appears that God made the sacrifice to end all sacrifices. He gave his only begotten Son, whose name was Jesus.

When Jesus died, He absorbed all the bad things we had done, and ended our need to sacrifice living things in the name of God.

It appears that Jesus rose from death to be with His loving Father in Heaven. This made it possible for us to also rise from our death to enter the kingdom of Heaven.

All we have to do is believe and ask Jesus to reside in our hearts. This, I'm told, will give us God's gift of eternal life.

It was really a big gift, from our almighty God, when He gave us his only Son.

He loved us so very much, and He made the ultimate sacrifice, so all of us could live in that beautiful place called Heaven.

Patricia A Fisher

Ya Know
I Just Might Be Christian

Ya know?
I just might be Christian.

Every time
That I pray

I always use
The word Jesus.

I like
To pray this way.

Ya know?
At the beginning,

When I was
Just a child,

I was baptized
Two different ways.

My parents
Were not reconciled!

Mom had me
Baptized Baptist.

Lutheran`
Was daddy's choice.

Just what I
Would believe in,

I never
Had a voice.

Patricia A Fisher

I learned
A lot of the music.

The hymns
Were so comforting.

One thing
I learned about churches,

At church,
They want you to sing!

So, I would
Sing my heart out –

Never
Heeding the words.

I never knew
What all of this meant.

But I sang
Just like the birds!

Because of
All of the fighting,

Around what faith
We would be,

I had much
Apprehension.

I never
Completely broke free!

So, some of the words
Like Christian,

Or sin,
Or being blessed,

Have the
Wrong connotation.

These words,
I never expressed!

Patricia A Fisher

So, I lived my life
Without them –

These words
I never said.

But I would still
Say my prayers,

Sometimes when
I went to bed.

So, later on
I explored

A different way
To believe.

I thought that
Everyone was God.

From this
I found no reprieve.

Things were ok
For awhile,

Living in
This way,

But there was
Something missing,

Which brings us
To this day.

Today, I still
Can't say those words

Without
A difficult time.

But I want
A Father in Heaven.

Is this
A terrible crime?

Patricia A Fisher

The only crime
That I can see

Is excluding
So many folks –

Saying,
"Ours is the only way.

There's Heaven
When one of us croaks."

This part
Has me worried.

Yet, a loving Father
I want.

A loving Father
In Heaven,

A warmer
Confidant…

I choose to
Look a bit closer,

To understand
The ways,

Of what to do
When you're Christian.

What happens
When someone prays?

We've come to
The main event,

Of what
A Christian has.

Faith is
What they believe in.

There's
No test to pass.

Patricia A Fisher

So, I am
Gonna try faith.

There's nothing
To conceal.

Ya know?
I just might be Christian.

Having faith
Seems to be real.

I don't have
To be perfect

In what
I do believe.

It's enough
To have faith,

And this
Is my reprieve...

An Unwelcome Guest

I do not want to change anyone's values. I just want to share how I empowered myself, when I could see no other way.

I think that evil won't go where there is a hefty dose of goodness. There just isn't room.

I was able to shorten my discomfort by putting evil in its' place. Its' place is nowhere in my heart, mind and spirit.

I have dedicated my life to love, truth and respect and, when humor comes, my life is complete.

So, this next piece I share with love in my heart. It is with hope that I will be of assistance, during the times you feel you have been overcome with bad feelings.

Writing My Way Out of Evil

How can I come back from being possessed by what has to be evil? It has only just come over me in the last hour or two, but even an hour or two is too much!

I called my therapist and she told me to fill my mind, once again, with why I am happier than I ever been in my life.

The words would not come, until I did other work first. I had to deal with the evil.

Evil, go away! You are hurting me again. Now I know it's you who gets me down, and makes me cry. Now I know it is you who possesses me, and makes me crash.

What's the matter? Do you feel lonesome? Do you need a good, kind person to accompany you in your ugliness? Do you want to erase all I have become?

Do you need to hurt people, and rip away the hope and joy from their hearts?

Patricia A Fisher

I've heard and believe, "An unwelcome guest flees from the scene." Evil, you are not welcome!

You must know how many tears you have brought unto innocent people, who are unaware of your power on earth. You drag us through the muck, to your door. As we enter, to late do we know where we are. We can only guess, by the pain in our hearts, and the illness in our bodies.

Well, I will tell you now, oh evil one. I am taking back my body, mind and spirit. These are my God–given gifts.

I will laugh and be happy. I'll be proud of myself again. I will do good, and be good, and I will praise my Heavenly Father. Every time I do this, it will be your cue to stay away from me.

Every time I have that inner smile, or see a beautiful sunset, I will be reminded that God is near and He loves me so very much.

I will know to keep my eye toward the good, and not succumb to the evil that is trying to take me away.

Patricia A Fisher

Dear Heavenly Father,
Help me to see.

People are limited
Just like me.

I have to learn
Deep down inside.

Nothing is worth
All the tears I have cried.

I must take it easy
From day to day.

None of us humans
Should live in this way.

When something happens,
And feels just like hell,

We are not coping
With life very well.

Taking things easy,
And letting them go,

Puts in perspective
Our feelings of woe.

Forcing our selves
To do happy things,

Puts us in touch
With fun that life brings.

Patricia A Fisher

SOMETIMES

I PUT GOD

ON

A PEDISTAL.

If we have forgiven someone we
might decide to put space
between us and them.

Forgiving someone does not
mean we will have fewer choices.

At times, forgiving can be quite
liberating as we gain peace of
mind.

Patricia A Fisher

Forgiving Oprah

If only
All the people
On this planet
Could forgive

Forgiveness
In itself
Would speak
To where we live

Speaking
Economically
We all can
Use this gift

From the richest
To the poorest
It gives us all
A lift

Now, there I was
Daydreaming
Of what
I am not sure

Suddenly
There was Oprah!
I suddenly
Thought of her

Somewhere
In my past
She shocked me
Just a little

She was out of
Character
Not fit as
A Fiddle

Patricia A Fisher

This night
Was an award night
A young girl
Smiled and smiled

So happy
To see Oprah
Her hair
Was cut and styled

Oprah walked
Toward her
So she could be
Announced

The young girl
Didn't skip a beat
When Oprah seemed
To pounce

This sweet
And innocent girl
Waiting for
A star

A star like
Oprah Winfrey
Someone
Who'd come far

The young girl
Introduced
Who launched
'O' Magazine

The long time
Top TV host
Was just a
Little mean

Patricia A Fisher

My mind took note
Of this happening
I never really
Forgot

How could Oprah
Act this way
By millions
She was caught

One day here
Years later
A title
Crossed my mind

I wrote
'Forgiving Oprah'
A person
Mostly kind

The Absence of Awful

That one little time
She was angry
I never saw this
Before

Oprah was being
Human
I'm probably
Doing it more

But you know
Through that forgiveness
My heart just
Mellowed out

I can see
More clearly
And I
Just have no doubt

Patricia A Fisher

That we are
Only human
The poorest
To the top

The Power
Of forgiveness
Makes discomfort
Stop

The power of
Forgiveness
Felt most by
Who forgives.

The person
Who's forgiven
May not know
He is

The person
Oprah Winfrey
With all the good
She's done

I still needed
To forgive
I feel good
When it's done.

The power of
Forgiveness
Straight across
The board

Is free
To everybody
Something
We afford

Patricia A Fisher

My other editor
Laura
Listened
For a spell

She said to me
Forgive myself
Write 'bout
That as well

Now here's
A point to ponder
About forgiving
Ourselves

Never did it
Come to me
From the place
Where goodness dwells

I've asked
My Heavenly Father
Forgive me
What I've done

I just haven't
Forgiven me
It could be
Somewhat fun

It seems
Forgiving Oprah
Was beyond
My comfort level

But then I thought
Forgiving myself
Could help me
Fight the devil

Patricia A Fisher

Thank you
Oprah Winfrey
This story
You inspire

Instead of
Criticizing you
I could escape
The mire

The Bible says
Forgive ourselves
Seventy
Times seven

I can be
Mischievous
And still
Get into Heaven

I could write
A story
What Laura
Said to me

About my own
Forgiveness
This will
Help me be

Laura is
My therapist
She caught
A big mistake

I'm letting Oprah
Off the hook
I've
Other fish to bake!

Patricia A Fisher

Our Dearest Oprah

I cried all the way through your interview with Whitney Houston. Days later I am crying again. I had to add this account of you two being lonely at the top. It was such a surreal moment where each of you spoke from your soul and led with your heart. This kind of moment doesn't happen often.

Oprah, I have written 12 books in the name of mental wellness. My Dennis and I published them privately with no marketing skills.

In my own way I have felt alone writing these books and practicing loving people with them. Many get what they need to live better lives.

They tell me that I describe feelings for which they have no words. They tell me thank you. It was very odd when my therapist quoted something I wrote years ago. I quickly told her it was mine. The quote was, 'acting as if'.

Acting long enough, as if everything is alright, eventually does make everything alright,

I realize the respect people get when you interview them. I also know that you must let your audience know the truth as I do.

You and Whitney really related and you both truly loved each other.

Do to that interview, Whitney's depth was made apparent and her beauty still knows no bounds. She said her gift came down from her mom through her to her daughter.

Whitney reached so deep inside for strength and she prayed to the Lord every day. When you both prayed at the same time the day of the interview, I was so moved.

Neither of you knew the other was praying.

Well, God bless you both. You have both made your limitless mark on the world...

Patricia A Fisher

God Didn't Say

Ouch! That hurt
For the hundredth time!
What did I do?
Was it a crime?

Did I hurt his feelings?
Did I turn my back?
When he needed something,
Were things out of whack?

I can't remember hurting him.
With an angry tone.
I can't remember calling names,
When we were all alone.

He tries to hurt me everyday
That we walk past each other.
I swear I have no choices
From one day to the other.

So now I feel frustration.
I want to end this now.
I tell myself, "I must be kind."
And then I make a vow.

I look into a bible.
Big as life it tells,
"Love one another."
Does this ring any bells?

In the book God tells us,
"Do love everyone,
And not only the easiest –
The people who are fun…"

My vow brought peace amazing,
Because of what I read.
"Love not just the easiest."
Is what the good book said.

Patricia A Fisher

They Call It Sin

I never have wanted
To say it –

This little word
So small.

Even though it's
A small word,

It might affect
Us all.

This little word called sin
Is hard for me to say.

I really cannot tell you
Why I feel this way.

It seems
The wages of sin

Are very grave
Indeed…

The wages of sin
Are death.

Yet my God
Knows my need.

He says, "If you
Live in the word

That I have
Shared with you,

You'll have life
Eternal,

And you'll have
Heaven too."

All I know
Is I have learned

That the devil
Is quite real!

He runs the Earth
By hurting folks,

And showing them
How to feel.

He wants us all
To feel rotten.

He wants us
To lie and cheat.

He causes a war
Inside us.

He's very hard
To beat.

I've decided
Here on this Earth

God just does
What He can.

Patricia A Fisher

What about his
Creation?

What about
Saving man?

Since evil rules
The Earth,

God can't always
Win.

It brings us back
To that strange little word,

That little word
Called sin...

The Absence of Awful

Desires of the devil
Are like trumpets loud and clear.

When God speaks, it's a whisper.
It takes away my fear.

He whispers words like 'love'.
He tells us, "Be of good cheer."

He says that just for the asking,
He will always be near.

He says one day we will see him
Just as clear as day.

He wants to take us to Heaven.
After we pass away...

Patricia A Fisher

If we ask forgiveness,
For mistakes that we have
made,

Like sins against our brother,
Our guilt begins to fade.

If we ask forgiveness
For acting against our self

This is one of the greatest sins
Says the good book on the shelf.

Every day we'll be stronger.
Sometimes we'll rejoice.

With Jesus as our savior,
We sort of have a choice.

Of whether we will suffer
For eternity

Or live forever in Heaven
With bliss as a certainty.

At the very beginning,
In the Garden of Eden they
were.

God created two people –
Two beautiful people for sure.

From the tree of good and evil,
They shared a bite to eat.

God had told them not to.
He told them not to cheat.

Patricia A Fisher

He said, "You may have this
garden.
So the story goes,

But the tree of good and evil
Was the only tree God chose.

He told sweet Eve and Adam,
"This is not your tree.

If you eat from this one,
The first sin there will be."

They ate from this forbidden
tree,
And learned 'bout evil and good.

That little word with so much
power
Proved they never should.

The Absence of Awful

Go against what God had said.
For He gave them a choice.

Yet man is man and God is God.
They ignored His mighty voice.

So Adam and Eve
Were made to leave

This garden
Where all was good.

Now they knew
About evil –

Like God had said
They would.

Patricia A Fisher

Later on Jesus was born,
And told to walk the Earth.

God had made him ready
Even before His birth.

So here He came all innocent –
Yet man He was as well.

He came to us so innocently
So we'd not go to hell…

He took on all our bad stuff
That we had done so long.

He absorbed our sinfulness –
All that we'd done wrong.

The Absence of Awful

Now we don't have to die,
Since He came to the Earth.

We can ask forgiveness,
Because of Jesus' birth.

We can have eternity
In Heaven – Don't you know?

'Cause God gave us his child
Two thousand years ago…

Patricia A Fisher

Dennis and I went to our eye doctor, who we call J.J. We always have a little fun when we go there. My first test was a great success. I was so happy!

Then Dr. J.J. said, "Now we need to do a second test."

I got scared, so I said, "I just remembered I have something cooking on the stove at home!"

At this point, we were all giggling, and that second test turned out perfectly.

Dear Sweet Master Of All

These days I come to you with thanks for my feelings of abundance. I close my eyes and drink the pure sweet music of my world.

I am amazed at your majesty!

I know you were pleased to have created us, for we are both limited and limitless. We are capable and profound.

I see that we have made most everything on the surface of our earth from the ground beneath our feet.

I am in awe at what you have put before us.

We have challenges to keep
ourselves occupied, and the
rewards of meeting those
challenges are endless.

We are capable of love, smiles,
tears, and caring for the less
fortunate. When someone falls,
there are others who come to
their aid.

I am honored, oh master of all,
for you have lead us this far.

Stay close within our reach for we
stumble and grope. Though
capable as we are, at times we
cry out in pain.

Let us know you are with us when all we see is darkness. At these times we miss you most of all.

Let us see that our pain is no less miraculous than our joy.

We thank you for our being able to love and to laugh, for these make our waiting for you possible.

Patricia A Fisher

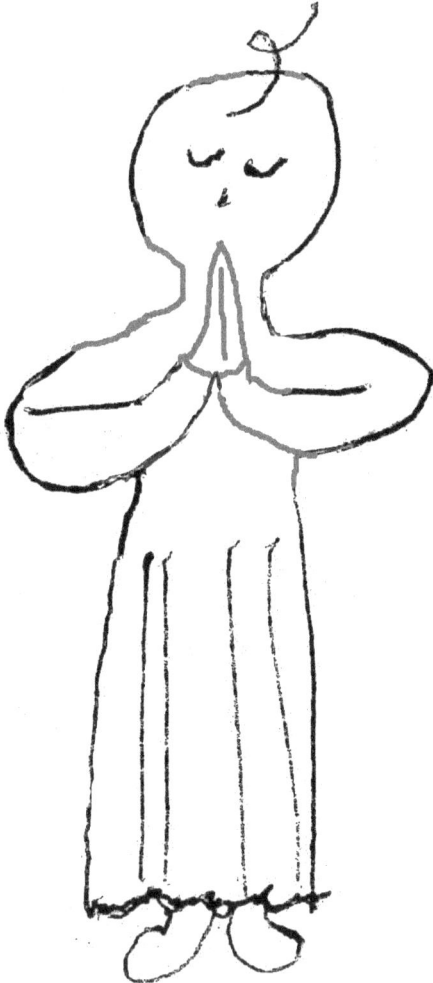

To be very, very great

you have to be

very, very

humble

My Dennis,
If I Should Die

Again I have loved you since before I met you. We have been married nearly 40 years and you are still and always an amazing man. You walk in the light of God, but you never preach about it.

People are never afraid of you as you have never been a threat to anyone (even mom).

My dear sweet love, my surgery is coming soon. I know you would miss me more than anyone. I love you more than my own life. We made a vow that we would be together for eternity. If I go first, we will meet in Heaven.

I don't think you have ever wasted time thinking of how to get back at me for something. You have loved me completely with your big beautiful heart.

We practice loving people. I think we do pretty well together. It has been our treat to the world for giving us so much. I am sure that having you in my life made it possible for me to write all of my books(more loving people). It is so neat how much they have helped people.

Sweet love, I can't say all that's in my heart for we have been together so long…

Thank you honey for all the times you have surprised me with something you've done for us or for me. You never bragged about it like I usually do. I'd be living life as usual and a lot of times I would find something you did that made me smile.

Thank you for helping me fight the demons. Thank you for comforting me when I cried, and for repeating what I've said in such a way it makes us both laugh.

Thank you God for bringing us both together. We each have given support to the other.

You are love as I've said many times. You are part of why I believe in truth, respect, love, and laughter.

Thanks for what you told me that I celebrate everything! I've realized that it's true. It was something my family never seemed to understand.

Well babe, if I go first, try to remember the fun we've had (like little Kris Kringle).

Please take good care of yourself and Kris. Keep reading Our Daily Bread and the Bible. Maybe go to church each Sunday. Get out with friends and family more or simply go by yourself. Or just do 'Dennis things'.

Patricia A Fisher

I pray that you have everything good. Although I get a little jealous thinking of you and a red head. (smile...)

Read your motor home magazines, you get a lot out of them.

God bless you and keep you,
All my love to you.

You're wife forever,
Patricia

The Greatest Love

Well, later I did die. Not all of me…

For forty three years, people have crowded me, poked and prodded me, and hurt me with their words.

I also feel hurt deeply when my family stays away so much.

Right now I only need this pen and paper to tell what just happened.

I knew I had enough of those people who guided me painfully to this day.

Patricia A Fisher

Today, I got extremely upset.
The phone didn't work. I knew
this was the last straw.

I went into a restroom and locked
the door. I turned off the lights.
There in the dark, I was
hysterical.

Then my therapist called. I
screamed at her that I hated
everybody!

Especially, after the last three
years of medical tests of all kinds,
and maybe six surgeries, I
screamed that I was crippled
mentally, physically, and
emotionally!

I found that I hated everyone but me.

For a change, I turned my rage outward instead of turning it back into myself. This was me finally loving me…

I was aware of this peaceful and innocent being, safe inside, as I raged outwardly.

Today, February 16, 2012, I began a new journey. This new journey ended the self blame I didn't know I had. It was replaced by self love.

Patricia A Fisher

Like the song says, "Learning to love yourself is the greatest love of all." (Sung by Whitney Houston)

So, there in the dark, with horrible pain, I passed through the fear and hate unscathed and innocent like a new born babe passing through the birth canal with all the rage in the world.

The Promise of Tomorrow

Outside, there is a roaring wind.
I am scared yet faithful.

I write as a tree branch crashes
on top of our motorhome (our
home).

I look out the window
and wonder about the
weather report that spoke of
hundred mile an hour winds.
I feel scared while hoping we will
be alright.

I feel full of unrest as another
blast of wind hits us and I
scream.

Patricia A Fisher

Our higher power may want us to
come home, which is ok.
We have really been in hell
for several years.

I have to say that I have no
power over this storm and no
power over a higher power.

I am releasing that evil
possession of my body, mind
and spirit. I am on a mission to
take care of them as they are the
temple of my innocence and a
vessel of God's love.

Is there a promise of tomorrow?
Is there a new day?
Will I be more patient of those
around me? Will I be more patient
with myself when things don't go
well for me?

My rage is like that roaring storm
outside—a vexation
to my spirit—a vexation to all
living things.

The storm is over now and we
have been spared again.

I question the promise of
tomorrow for all we can promise
ourselves is this moment.

We can be secure when we can
say, "I am alright right now."

When I am in the moment there
is a calming presence. It is like
watching the movie that is life.

All of us are warriors fighting for
life. We pray for the possibility
that there really is the promise of
a brand new tomorrow...

Patricia A Fisher

A Silent Warrior

Dennis and I had to give Kris away, our beautiful, sweet, and funny Kris... We loved him so very much. He was our puppy.

I've cried more about losing Kris than I have any human being.

Being ill ourselves, we couldn't take care of him as well as we would have liked. He became real sick and it would have cost thousands for an operation he needed.

His little arteries were not delivering blood to his liver for processing. They were going around it instead. So the vet told us the terrible news.

We relinquished him to a woman who has a lot of animals in her home. She also loved him the moment she saw him. She told us that she could care for him at a lower cost because she worked at the animal hospital where we were.

Here come the tears again. Will they ever stop?

My Dennis rarely use to cry or even talk about losses or other sad happenings. He would find something to do such as reading, TV, or working on one of his projects.

This went on for a long time. I would talk or cry and he would listen, but giving Kris away made Dennis cry for a long time. We were both hit pretty hard. That little dog taught us a lot, and we will never forget him.

In my youth I hardly ever cried. I was the one who listened to everyone. I usually led any conversation by asking good questions. I thought I was in control, but actually I was invisible.

Then I was told that I had a right to be heard. I find that I look forward to giving more speeches. Along with helping people, being heard is still very important to me.

My Dennis still can't think back to what has caused him distress. I usually just hold him and ask him questions about the last couple of days. Sometimes this works to bring answers, and he feels much better. When he cries I don't think there are enough tears for all the pain he is in.

After forty years of marriage I still wonder if Dennis just handles things differently. He says he does.

When I worry, at times he will say, "What's the use wasting time and energy when there is nothing we can do about it?" He really means it!

This may be one reason why he seems so strong.

He always has time and energy for me. I have to be careful comparing myself to him because he is so good, and he wins every time.

He tells me to compare myself to myself. It doesn't make sense to compare yourself to others.

I was so quiet until about the age of twenty. This is when I started therapy.

When I started talking, I just never stopped. Dennis didn't have a chance! From the day we met I talked and he listened. Silently he listened...

He still listens, and I still talk. I even became an author I had so much to say.

Dennis hears every story I write as soon as it is finished. He sometimes edits my work.

My Dennis says a lot with very few words. He, too, is a warrior like me, but he has little to say.

It appears that I am a noisy warrior and I have been visible for forty three years. Dennis is part of that.

He is not noisy. He is not mean. Dennis is, and always has been, 'A Silent Warrior'.

Patricia A Fisher

Yeah, Yeah, Yeah,

But

What

About

_ME???_

D. H. Fisher

Patricia A Fisher

The Absence of Awful

.

www.ingramcontent.com/pod-product-compliance
Lightning Source LLC
Chambersburg PA
CBHW062200270326
41930CB00009B/1599